Somebodyness

A Workbook to Help Kids Boost Their Self-Confidence

If you're reading this book, you may be feeling a little down on yourself. Maybe you've been bullied or picked on. Maybe other kids have laughed at you, or made you feel very small.

It's easy to let these things get you down and make you feel like you're not special or important, but you know what? YOU ARE a wonderful person! You have a lot *of* special qualities and talents that make you who you are. As you complete the activities in this book, you'll learn what those special qualities are. You'll also learn to remind yourself of how special and wonderful you are!

Take a second to introduce yourself.

Hi! My name is _____.

I have _____ hair, _____ eyes, and _____skin.

My favorite color is _____.

and my favorite food is _____.

At school, my favorite subject is _____.

At home, my favorite activity is _____.

In the box below, draw a picture of yourself. If you want, you can include some of your favorite things in the picture as well.   .

Now think about your feelings and fill in the following sentences:

I feel happy when…

_____

_____

I feel sad when…

_____

_____

I feel important when…

_____

_____

I feel angry when…

_____

_____

I feel loved when…

_____

_____

I feel disappointed when…

_____

_____

I feel frustrated when…

_____

_____

A warm fuzzy is something good that happens. A cold prickly is something bad that happens. Read the situations below. Color the warm fuzzies yellow and the cold pricklies gray.

Sara calls you a baby.

Will says you're a good friend.

Cullen laughs when you fall.

Erica gives back a dollar that you dropped.

Josh hits you.

Erin says she likes your poster.

Your mom gives you a hug.

Laurel takes your lunch money.

Quince stops being your friend.

How would the warm fuzzies make you feel?

_____

_____

How would the cold pricklies make you feel?

_____

_____

Think about what has happened over the last week. Come up with three warm fuzzies and three cold pricklies that happened to you, or that you gave to others.

Knowing how you feel and when you feel that way can help you become more self-confident and feel better about yourself. Each of the circles below is labeled with an emotion. Draw a face in the circle to represent the emotion listed, and on the lines below the emotion, write how you know you're feeling that emotion.

ANGRY

_____
_____
_____

HAPPY

_____
_____
_____

SAD

_____
_____
_____

LOVED

_____
_____
_____

DISAPPOINTED

_____
_____
_____

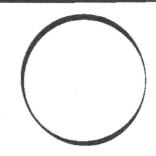

IMPORTANT

_____
_____
_____

The words below are adjectives. Adjectives are describing words, and we often use adjectives to describe people. The adjectives in the lightning bolts are negative adjectives, and not nice ways to describe people. The adjectives in the stars are positive adjectives, and nice ways to describe people. Look at the adjectives, and color in the ones people have used to describe you.

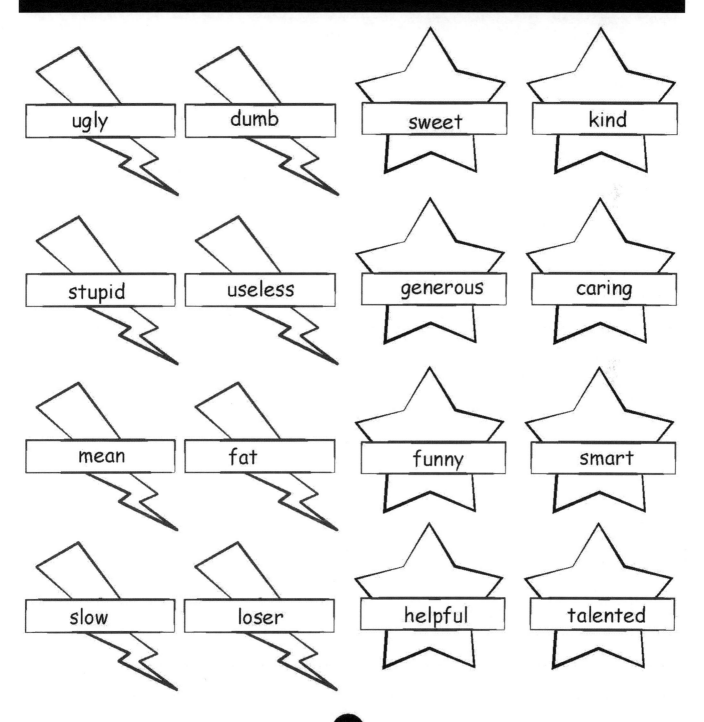

Think about the negative adjectives you colored in.

Have you ever been called any other negative names? If so, list them on the lines below.

_____

_____

How does it make you feel when people use negative names or adjectives to describe you?

_____

_____

_____

Think about the positive adjectives you colored in.

Have you ever been called any other positive adjectives? If so, list them on the lines below.

_____

_____

How does it make you feel when people use positive adjectives to describe you?

_____

_____

_____

Think about a time when someone called you a negative name or said something bad about you. Draw a picture of it in the box below.

Describe what is happening in the picture:

_____

_____

_____

How did you feel when that happened?

_____

_____

_____

What do you do when someone calls you a negative name?

_____

_____

_____

Now think of three or four things you could do instead of that.

_____

_____

_____

When people call you negative names or say bad things about you, you can choose to get angry, cry, and let them get to you...OR you can choose to ignore them, walk away, tell an adult, or turn the situation into something positive.

If a kid comes up to you and tells you that you're ugly, what's a positive way you can respond?

_____

_____

If a kid comes up to you and hits you, what's a positive way you can respond?

_____

_____

It's easier to keep bad things from affecting you when you feel good about yourself. What words do you use to describe yourself? Write them in the circles below.

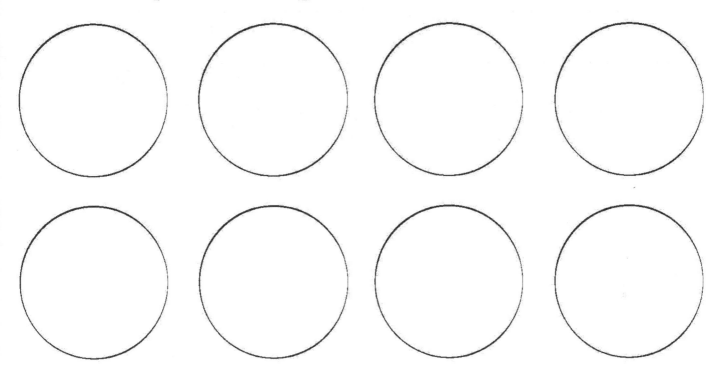

Look at the words above. Draw a line through all the circles with negative words in them. Use the positive words in the circles to fill in the sentence below. If you don't have enough positive words in the circles to finish the sentence, try hard to come up with some.

My name is _____

_____

and I am _____

_____

_____

and _____.

Think about the positive words you'd use to describe yourself. In the box below, draw a picture that shows a time when you felt like one of those words (for example, a time when you felt pretty or handsome).

When I Felt _____

Describe what is happening in the picture:

_____

_____

_____

Why did you feel that way in that moment?

_____

_____

_____

Sometimes, people will call you negative names or say bad things about you. When they do, it can help to remember the positive things about you. Negative words are like arrows, and positive words are like shields to prevent those arrows from hurting you! In the arrows below are negative things people might say to you. In each shield, write a positive word or phrase to block the arrow!

13

Think about the people in your life who love you or are your friends. Write their names on the lines below: _____

_____

_____

Now think about why those people love you. They don't love you because they have to — they love you because they see a lot of great things in you.

My family members and friends love me because... _____

_____

_____

_____

_____

_____

_____

_____

Doesn't it feel good to think about all the reasons people love you?

Something you're good at is called a strength. Knowing what you're good at can help you feel better when you encounter things you're not so good at, or that are hard. On the lines below, list five things you're good at.

1. _____
2. _____
3. _____
4. _____
5. _____

How do you know you're good at these things? Circle the reasons below.

I feel good when I do them.

People have told me I'm good at them.

They come easily to me.

I enjoy doing them.

People give me awards for doing them.

I feel excited about doing them.

Doing them makes me happy.

People like me because I can do them.

I teach others how to do them.

I use positive words when I talk about them.

Take the things you are good at, the reasons people love you, and the positive words you'd use to describe yourself. Decorate the shield below with those reasons, positive words, and strengths!

_____ 's Shield

In your life, you have a lot of responsibility: YOU get to decide your likes and dislikes, and how certain things make you feel. Look at the decisions in the left-hand column below. Decide who gets to make them by circling the appropriate word in the right-hand column.

What books I check out at the library…	ME	MY FRIENDS	ADULTS
What I put on in the morning…	ME	MY FRIENDS	ADULTS
Where I go to school…	ME	MY FRIENDS	ADULTS
What my favorite color is…	ME	MY FRIENDS	ADULTS
Who my friends are…	ME	MY FRIENDS	ADULTS
What I study in school…	ME	MY FRIENDS	ADULTS
Whom I like/don't like…	ME	MY FRIENDS	ADULTS
Whether I want to watch TV or play a game…	ME	MY FRIENDS	ADULTS
How I feel about something…	ME	MY FRIENDS	ADULTS
How I feel about myself…	ME	MY FRIENDS	ADULTS

Why shouldn't you let others determine how you feel? _____

_____

_____

Think about the times people have called you negative names or made you feel bad. Below, color in all the things you do when this happens.

cry	get angry	fight
punch something	yell	scream
kick something	lose your temper	say something back

These are all negative ways to handle the situation. When you react in these ways, you're letting other people decide how you're going to feel. Instead of reacting in those ways, fill in the boxes below with other ways you can respond by deciding not to feel bad about it.

talk to them	tell an adult	ignore them
journal	listen to music	walk away
take deep breaths	agree to disagree	_____

Sometimes kids and adults say and do things that aren't very nice, but they don't realize they're making you feel bad. Telling them how you feel can help them realize that what they said or did hurt you, and may keep them from doing it again. When you tell people how they made you feel, you can use something called an "I statement" or an "I message."

An "I statement" or "I message" looks like this:

When you _____ , I felt _____ .

Think about a time someone called you a mean name, and pretend to tell them about it by filling in the "I statement" below:

When you _____ , I felt _____ .

Now think about a time someone you love hurt your feelings or disappointed you, and fill in the "I statement" below:

When you _____ , I felt _____ .

What are two things that happened recently where you could've used an "I statement" or "I message"?

1. _____

_____

2. _____

_____

Other people aren't the only ones who can bring negative thoughts and feelings into your life. Sometimes, when things are hard or you aren't good at something, you can have your own negative feelings.

What is something that's hard for you to do?

_____

_____

Circle all the words below that describe how you feel when you try to do that hard thing.

ANGRY	FRUSTRATED	TIRED	DISAPPOINTED
WEAK	NOT GOOD ENOUGH	STUPID	DUMB
LAZY	DIFFERENT	UNCOOL	MAD
DEFEATED	WORTHLESS	NO GOOD	BAD
DISCOURAGED	CLUMSY	CLUELESS	AWFUL
EMBARRASSED	SAD	HOPELESS	INVISIBLE
ANNOYED	AFRAID	DEPRESSED	ROTTEN
SLOW			

Why do you think you feel that way?

_____

_____

Something you aren't good at is called a weakness. On the lines below, list five of your weaknesses.

1. _____

2. _____

3. _____

4. _____

5. _____

How do you know you aren't good at these things? Circle all the reasons below.

People tell me I'm not good at them.

I don't like doing them.

They're hard for me to do.

I feel awkward when I do them.

They make me feel stupid.

They take a lot of effort.

I get upset when I have to do them.

People make fun of me when I do them.

I feel like I can't do them.

I feel hopeless when I do them.

When you try to do something hard, you can start to feel very negative about yourself. However, you don't have to feel that way! Instead of feeling something negative, you can try to turn the way you're feeling into something more positive.

Remember when you listed your weaknesses? List them again here:

1. _____

2. _____

3. _____

4. _____

5. _____

When you think about these weaknesses, you usually say, "I can't do it."

The first step to thinking positively about your weaknesses is to stop saying you can't and start saying you can. Turn each weakness listed above into an "I can" statement below.

1. I can _____.

2. I can _____.

3. I can _____.

4. I can _____

5. I can _____

How do you think saying "I can" instead of "I can't" do something will make you feel better about it?

_____

_____

_____

Sometimes, when people aren't good at something, they VISUALIZE themselves doing it well. This means they create a picture in their mind of them doing it well.

Before you visualize, think about something you're good at:

I'm good at _____ .

Circle all the words that describe how you feel when you do the thing you're good at:

HAPPY	EXCITED	MOTIVATED	IMPORTANT	CONFIDENT	FREE
ENCOURAGED	SPECIAL	RESPONSIBLE	GOOD	ALIVE	PRETTY
SATISFIED	AWESOME	CALM	SMILEY	FUN	
HANDSOME	CHEERFUL	GLAD	AMAZING	BRAVE	

Why do you think you feel this way?

_____

_____

_____

_____

_____

Now that you've remembered what it feels like when you do something good: It's time to visualize. Think about something that's hard for you to do and write it on the line below:

_____ is hard for me to do.

Now, visualize you doing the hard thing. Take the picture from your mind, and try to draw it in the box below.

Another way to feel better about something you're not very good at is to make it easier to do. For example, if you feel bad because you can't read an entire book, you can break this task into smaller goals. For example, your first goal could be to read a sentence in the book. Think about the thing that's hard for you to do that you wrote about and drew a picture of on the previous page.

Why is it hard for you to do?

_____

_____

_____

What's one thing you could do to make it easier? How could you turn it into a smaller goal?

_____

_____

_____

_____

By breaking something hard into smaller pieces, you increase your chances of success. It also may not seem as hard once it's broken down!

Instead of feeling angry, frustrated, mad, helpless, stupid, or other negative emotions, think of other ways to handle difficult situations. Fill in the sentences below with situations you find difficult, along with two ways you can handle each of them better.

When _____

I can _____

or _____ .

When _____

I can _____

or _____ .

When _____

I can _____

or _____ .

When _____

I can _____

or _____ .

Sometimes, no matter how hard you try, you still can't do some of the things that are hard for you. THAT'S OKAY. There are still a lot of things you can do really well!

1.   What's one thing you do really well?

_____

_____

2.   What's something you do even better than that?

_____

_____

3.   What's something you recently learned how to do?

_____

_____

4.   What's something you can do that you're proud of?

_____

_____

5.   What's one thing you're not afraid of doing?

_____

_____

You're good at a lot of things, and those things are positives!
Think about all the things you're good at. How can you use those things to help other people? Brainstorm examples of how you can help others by filling in the thought bubbles below.

Maybe there are things you want to do or ways you could help others, but you don't have the courage. That's okay — being afraid is normal! What are some things you're afraid of doing? Why are you afraid of them? Fill in the chart below to answer these questions.

I AM AFRAID OF...	BECAUSE...

Getting over your fears requires being brave.

What does it mean to be brave?

_____

_____

Describe a time when you or someone you know was brave.

_____

_____

_____

_____

_____

_____

_____

Some of the bravest characters are superheroes.

Do you have a favorite superhero?

_____

_____

If you were a superhero, what would your superpower be?

_____

_____

 Draw a picture of yourself as a superhero.

Now that you've seen yourself as a superhero, it's time to start thinking about being brave. Choose one of the things you're afraid of, and fill in the sentence below.

I am afraid of ─────────────────────────────

because ──────────────────────────── .

Draw a picture of yourself being afraid.

 Now, draw picture of yourself conquering your fear!

Conquering your fears requires being brave.

One way I can be brave is by _____

_____

_____

_____.

It also requires coming up with a plan. In the boxes below, write the steps you'll take to be brave and overcome your fear.

It may take some time, but by being brave, you can start to overcome your fears. Now that you've learned more about yourself and how you feel, answer the following prompts.

My name is _____.

Three positive words to describe me are...

1. _____

2. _____

3. _____

When people are mean or say something negative to me, I will...

_____

_____

My greatest strengths are...

_____

_____

I can improve myself by...

_____

_____

Pretend someone is going to give you an award. Design it in the box below.

Describe the award, and why you've received it:

_____

_____

_____

_____

There's going to be a ceremony to present you with the award! You've been asked to come up to the stage and give an acceptance speech. In your speech, you must:

- Thank those who gave you the award
- Thank the people who helped you achieve the award
- Explain how you earned/why you deserve the award

Write your acceptance speech on the lines below:

_____

_____

_____

_____

_____

_____

_____

_____

_____

_____

Now that you've completed this workbook, use it as a reminder to help you be STRONG, CONFIDENT, and BRAVE. Pick it up when someone makes you feel bad, or when you're just feeling down, and let it remind you of how wonderful you really are!

Somebodyness: A Workbook to Help Kids Improve Their Self-Confidence

Text copyright © 2014 by Erainna Winnett, Ed.S.

Book Cover Design copyright © 2014 by Lucia Martinez

www.counselingwithheart.com

ISBN-10:0615983634

BISAC: Juvenile Nonfiction / Social Issues / Self-Esteem & Self-Reliance

Printed in the United States of America

Made in the USA
San Bernardino, CA
20 January 2018